CHI

FRIENDS
OF ACPL

Buddy BOOKS
Prehistoric Animals

American
Mastodon

ABDO
Publishing Company

A Buddy Book
by
Michael P. Goecke

VISIT US AT
www.abdopub.com

Published by Buddy Books, an imprint of ABDO Publishing Company, 4940 Viking Drive, Edina, Minnesota 55435. Copyright © 2004 by Abdo Consulting Group, Inc. International copyrights reserved in all countries. No part of this book may be reproduced in any form without written permission from the publisher.

Printed in the United States.

Edited by: Christy DeVillier
Contributing Editor: Matt Ray
Graphic Design: Deborah Coldiron
Image Research: Deborah Coldiron
Illustrations: Deborah Coldiron, Denise Esner
Photographs: Corel, Hulton Archives, Steve McHugh

Library of Congress Cataloging-in-Publication Data

Goecke, Michael P., 1968-
     American mastodon / Michael P. Goecke.
        p. cm. — (Prehistoric animals. Set II)
     Summary: Introduces the physical characteristics, habitat, and behavior of this prehistoric relative of modern-day elephants.
     Includes bibliographical references and index.
     ISBN 1-57765-973-2
     1. Mastodon—Juvenile literature. [1. Mastodon. 2. Mammals, Fossil. 3. Prehistoric animals. 4. Paleontology.] I. Title.

QE882.U7 G63 2003
569'.67—dc21
                                                          2002032276

Table of Contents

Prehistoric Animals

Dinosaurs are a famous group of prehistoric animals. They died out about 65 million years ago. Many exciting prehistoric animals lived after the dinosaurs. Some of them were saber-toothed cats, giant sloths, and woolly mammoths.

Scientists study fossils from prehistoric animals. Fossils help them understand what these exciting animals were like.

Dinosaurs are prehistoric animals.

Prehistoric Animals

5

The American Mastodon

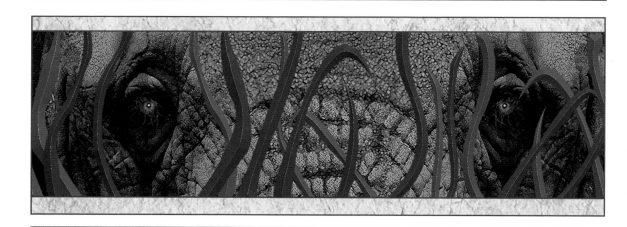

American Mastodon
(uh-MER-uh-cun MAS-tuh-don)

The American mastodon was a **prehistoric** elephant. It was one of the biggest land animals of its time. American mastodons lived in North America for about three million years.

The American mastodon was a prehistoric elephant.

7

The American mastodon was about as big as today's elephants. Adult males grew to become about nine feet (three m) tall. They weighed about six tons (five t). Female mastodons were smaller.

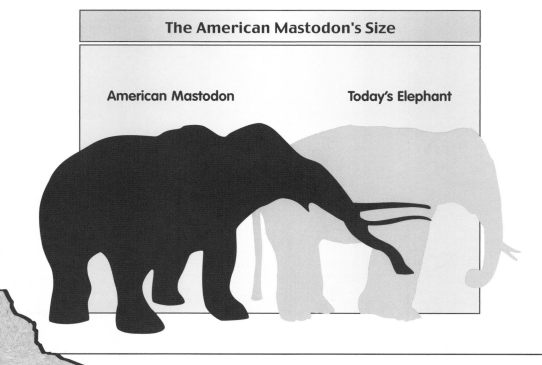

The American Mastodon's Size

American Mastodon   Today's Elephant

The American mastodon had a brown, hairy coat. It had strong shoulders, thick legs, and small ears. Like elephants today, the American mastodon also had a trunk.

All elephants have a trunk.

9

American Mastodon   Today's Elephant

The American mastodon's tusks grew longer
than the tusks of today's elephants.

American mastodons grew long
tusks. A male's tusks could grow to
become seven feet (two m) long. Today's
elephants have shorter tusks.

Fun Facts

Indian Elephants

Indian elephants live in southern Asia. They are the American mastodon's closest living relatives.

Indian elephants are smaller than African elephants. They have smaller ears, too. A male Indian elephant's **tusks** grow to become about six feet (two m) long. The females do not grow tusks.

This Indian elephant is related to the American mastodon.

Eating And Teeth

The American mastodon ate plants. It ate from larch, spruce, pine, and cedar trees. It probably ate grasses, mosses, and swamp plants, too.

The American mastodon crushed food between its large teeth. This **prehistoric** elephant had two upper teeth and two lower teeth. Each tooth was about the size of a shoebox.

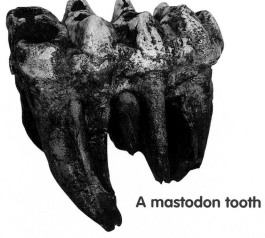

A mastodon tooth

Most elephants have flat teeth with ridges. The American mastodon's teeth were different. Their teeth had points called cusps. Teeth with cusps allowed them to chew tough, woody plants.

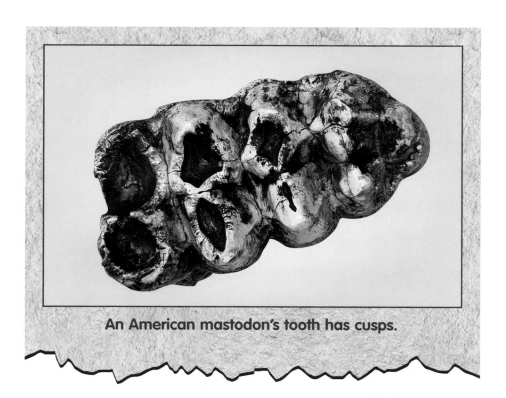

An American mastodon's tooth has cusps.

Like today's elephants, the American mastodon grew new teeth to replace old ones. It could grow six sets of teeth in its lifetime.

What did the American mastodon use its tusks for? Scientists believe they used their tusks to gather food. Maybe they broke off tree branches with their tusks. Tusks would help them break tree branches into bite-size pieces.

An Elephant's Trunk

Elephants use their trunks for eating, drinking, smelling, and bathing. American mastodons probably used their trunks for the same things.

An elephant's trunk can move in many ways. At the tip of an elephant's trunk are one or two "fingers." They help elephants grab and pick up things.

Elephants use their trunks to eat.

15

Scientists have names for important time periods in Earth's history. The time period that began about two million years ago is called the Pleistocene. American mastodons lived before, during, and after the Pleistocene.

The last Ice Age took place during the Pleistocene. During the Ice Age, parts of the world became very cold. Giant sheets of ice covered many lands.

The Pleistocene World

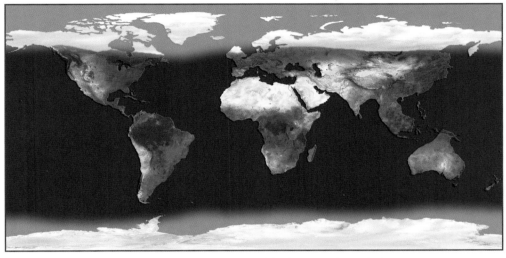

Ice covered parts of the world during the Pleistocene.

American mastodons lived all over North America. Some lived as far north as Alaska. Others lived as far south as Mexico. Scientists believe they lived in forests and near wet areas.

17

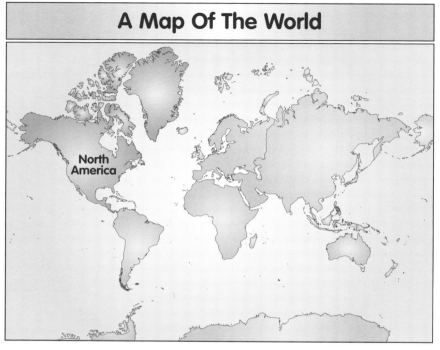

A Map Of The World

North
America

American mastodon fossils have been found in
North America.

American mastodons probably lived
among beavers, moose, horses, and
scimitar cats. Prehistoric people were
probably around, too. They may have
found ways to kill American mastodons
for food.

American mastodons died out about 10,000 years ago. Did a great climate change kill the plants it ate? Did prehistoric people hunt them to death? Today's scientists are not sure why American mastodons died out. Discovering more mastodon fossils may help them solve this mystery.

First Fossils

Charles Willson Peale was an American artist. He also enjoyed studying nature and new scientific discoveries. Peale opened the first natural history museum in America.

In 1801, Peale heard about some fossils found in Newburgh, New York. These fossils were very big bones. People thought the bones belonged to a giant mammoth. Mammoths were prehistoric elephants.

Charles Willson Peale

Peale went to Newburgh and dug up more bone fossils. He found two skeletons. He sent copies of the bones to Georges Cuvier. Cuvier was a French scientist.

A fossil of the American mastodon's tooth.

Cuvier said the bigger skeleton was not a mammoth. It had different teeth from the mammoths he knew about. Cuvier gave the unknown animal a new name. He called it a mastodon.

Important Words

climate the weather of a place over time.

cusps points on teeth.

fossil remains of very old animals and plants commonly found in the ground. A fossil can be a bone, a footprint, or any trace of life.

Ice Age a period in Earth's history when ice covered parts of the world. The last Ice Age ended about 11,500 years ago.

prehistoric describes anything that was around more than 5,500 years ago.

tusks large teeth that stick out of an animal's mouth.

Web Sites

To learn more about the American mastodon, visit ABDO Publishing Company on the World Wide Web. Web sites about the American mastodon are featured on our Book Links page. These links are routinely monitored and updated to provide the most current information available.

www.abdopub.com

23

Index

24